Deadliest Dinosaurs

Don Nardo

D1288637

ReferencePoint
Press®

San Diego, CA

© 2017 ReferencePoint Press, Inc.
Printed in the United States

For more information, contact:
ReferencePoint Press, Inc.
PO Box 27779
San Diego, CA 92198
www. ReferencePointPress.com

LIBRARY OF CONGRESS CATALOGING-IN-PUBLICATION DATA

Names: Nardo, Don, 1947-
Title: Deadliest dinosaurs / by Don Nardo.
Description: San Diego, CA : ReferencePoint Press, Inc., 2017. | Series:
    Deadliest predators | Audience: Grade 9 to 12.- | Includes bibliographical
    references and index.
Identifiers: LCCN 2016004075 (print) | LCCN 2016014010 (ebook) | ISBN
    9781682820483 (hardback) | ISBN 9781682820490 (eBook)
Subjects: LCSH: Dinosaurs--Juvenile literature.
Classification: LCC QE861.5 .N335 2017 (print) | LCC QE861.5 (ebook) | DDC
    567.9--dc23
LC record available at http://lccn.loc.gov/2016004075

Contents

Terrors of the Land, Seas, and Air

Long, long ago, in an era now lost in the deep mists of time, truly terrifying, nightmarish monsters existed on Earth. Beasts capable of crushing bones and stripping flesh in mere seconds dwelled on every continent. They inhabited all of nature's niches, or diverse separate settings. Some roamed the plains, forests, and hills on the land surfaces, while others hunted in the seas, lakes, and rivers. Still others stalked their prey in the skies overhead. Whichever niche they dominated, these frightening creatures literally ruled the world between 225 million and 65 million years ago.

Predators and Prey

The words *hunted* and *stalked* are crucial when looking back at these monsters. This is because they were all predators, meaning that they stalked and hunted other animals. They were also carnivorous, or meat-eating, because they survived by consuming the flesh of their prey. Among those prey were numerous kinds of herbivores, or plant eaters. Often heavy, fleshy, and slow moving, they were natural and frequent food supplies for the predators, although the meat eaters sometimes also turned on their own kind.

Of the leading predators in that long-ago era, many were dinosaurs. *Dinosaur* is a term scientists employ to describe a specialized kind of reptile-like land creature that is now largely extinct. A dinosaur walked or ran with its legs directly beneath its body, and thanks to that posture, it carried its belly and tail well off the ground. In comparison, most reptiles and amphibians walk with their bellies and tails dragging on the ground. Because the predatory dinosaurs dominated and in a sense ruled the world between 225 million and 65 million years ago, that era is frequently called the "age of the dinosaurs."

Yet even as the dinosaurian predators were the terrors of the land surfaces, other dangerous predators stalked their prey in the seas and skies. They were what modern experts sometimes call "dinosaur competitors," which most people tend to informally lump together with the dinosaurs. But no matter how one chooses to classify the predators of that age, one thing is certain. Namely, herbivores and other nonpredators lived in fear of those hungry hunters.

A Prehistoric Bloodbath

Another informal manner of seeing dinosaurs today—particularly predators like the famous *T. rex* (short for *Tyrannosaurus rex*)—is as the "bad guys" in popular novels and movies. Typically, these fearsome beasts are shown chasing, terrorizing, or eating horrified humans. For instance, Scottish writer Sir Arthur Conan Doyle's 1912 novel *The Lost World* spawned at least fourteen radio, television, and movie versions, the most recent of which was released in 2011. The story follows a group of modern explorers who find numerous dinosaur species living on a remote plateau in South America.

Predatory dinosaurs, capable of crushing bones and stripping flesh in mere seconds, dominated the earth many millions of years ago. They terrorized all other animals that lived during this long-ago era.

Although such works are highly entertaining, they are completely fictional. The vast majority of dinosaurs went extinct 65 million years ago, long before human beings evolved from small, tree-dwelling mammals. (The single dinosaurian group that survived the mass extinction was the one that led to modern birds.)

Thus, the earliest people on the planet never had to compete with or fight off attacks by huge predatory dinosaurs like *T. rex* and the even bigger *Spinosaurus*. Those monsters were able to devour a human-sized animal in a couple of tasty bites. Nor did the first humans face creatures like the smaller but no less deadly *Troodon.* Somewhat smaller than a person, it could run far faster than a human, and like the first people, it was smart enough to engage in pack hunting. *Had* people and such predatory dinosaurs coexisted, most scientists agree that there would likely have been a prehistoric bloodbath that fledgling humanity would not have survived.

Chapter 1

Tyrannosaurus Rex

In the popular, exciting 1993 film *Jurassic Park*, scientist Dr. Alan Grant (played by Sam Neill) and two adventurous children find themselves stalked by a giant killer. Huddling together on a muddy dirt road at night in the rain, the three sit as still as possible. Clearly, they hope the mighty *T. rex* will not detect them and turn them into its evening meal. Fortunately for them, the monster's eyesight is not very good, and instinct has taught it to react to the movement of prey animals. So after a few seconds, it turns its attention elsewhere, just long enough for the terrified people to escape.

Indeed, paleontologists—experts on very ancient life forms—say that this fictional account likely mirrors the reactions of some of the prey of the real *T. rex* long ago. Most creatures probably could not outrun the towering beast. So any unfortunate ones it cornered must have frozen in place and hoped they would escape its notice. Then as now in nature's ongoing drama between predators and prey, some of the *T. rex*'s quarry did manage to get away. But others ended up dying in its enormous jaws.

A Well-Deserved Royal Title

This was the brutal way of things in most of what is now North America during the Late Cretaceous period, lasting from about 99 million to 65 million years ago. During those years, says dinosaur researcher Cavan Scott, there emerged "hunters the likes of which the Earth had never seen before." Called the tyrannosaurids, they were "a group of predators that took bloodthirsty killing to a new level."[1]

Tyrannosaurid is the scientific name of one of several families within a larger group of dinosaurs called theropods. All theropods were bipeds, meaning they walked and ran on two legs, as humans do. Also, theropods had forelimbs—arms—that were shorter than their legs, and nearly all of them were deadly predators with sizable jaws filled with extremely sharp teeth.

Caught in the enormous jaws of a T. rex *(pictured), prey animals had little chance to escape. Exceptionally sharp teeth and a crushing bite gave* T. rex *the advantage over most other creatures.*

TYRANNOSAURUS REX AT A GLANCE

- **Scientific name:** *Tyrannosaurus rex*
- **Scientific suborder:** Theropod
- **Scientific family:** Tyrannosaurid
- **Range:** North America
- **Habitat:** Well-watered forests, lowland plains, and swamplands
- **Average size:** 40 feet (12 m)
- **Diet:** The flesh of any animal it could catch or scavenge
- **Life span:** Uncertain, but possibly about thirty years
- **Key features:** Enormous thighs; large jaw with many big teeth
- **Deadly because:** Fast, powerful; massive, bone-crushing bite

Theropods lived all around the globe and came in all sizes. Some were the size of chickens, whereas others were human sized or bigger. Over time, one family of theropods that lived in North America—the tyrannosaurids—grew unusually large. Of the several tyrannosaurid species, the biggest of all was *Tyrannosaurus rex*, a Latin term roughly translating as "king of the tyrant lizards." The *T. rex* certainly deserved its royal title. In part this was because it was physically imposing. From its nose to the tip of its tale, an adult measured some 40 feet (12 m), the length of an average modern house. A grown *T. rex* was also very heavy. As a kind of general shorthand, paleontologists sometimes use the term *elephant sized* to describe some of the larger predatory dinosaurs. An adult African elephant weighs about 6 tons (5.4 metric tons), and that is also the estimated weight of a full-grown *T. rex*.

Stalking and Capture

A *T. rex*'s great size was not the only trait that made it a fearsome predator. Another physical advantage it possessed was its speed, which was related to the size and degree of muscularity of its legs. Paleontologists have found more than fifty complete and partial *T. rex* skeletons, and close studies of the legs indicate the size and placement of the original muscles. Clearly, the beast had enormous, very muscular thighs. Many experts contend that these allowed it to spring forward rapidly and to run fast. The exact speed that a *T. rex* could run is unknown. Scientific estimates range from as low as 11 miles per hour (17.7 kph) to as high as 40 miles per hour (64.4 kph).

Whatever this dinosaur's top speed, some evidence suggests that it may have needed to attain such a high rate of movement for only short distances. A number of scientists think this is because *T. rex* likely displayed a kind of hunting behavior similar to that of today's top predators in the wild—lions and other big carnivorous cats. More often than not, lions carefully stalk their prey for quite a while before going into attack mode at a full run.

In such steady, patient stalking behavior, a lion observes and matches the speed and direction of its moving prey. "A carnivore on the attack," scientist James O. Farlow explains, "will usually adjust its stride until it comes into exact rhythm" with the animal it intends to attack. A lion, cheetah, or other big hunter-cat, Farlow adds, slowly speeds up "until it has caught up with its target. The predator then changes the length of its stride to match that of its prey."[2] Using this strategy, the predator significantly reduces the distance it has to cover when it does break into a full run. It can therefore pour all available energy into a short, very quick sprint, maximizing its chances of successfully catching the prey.

Farlow and many other modern experts think that large predatory dinosaurs like *T. rex* stalked prey the same way. One strong piece of evidence for this is a set of ancient dinosaur tracks discovered in 1940 on the banks of the Paluxy River in central Texas. The numerous tracks, together called a trackway, preserved the various steps in an actual stalking and capture of a large herbivore called *Pleurocoelus.* The attacker was an *Acrocanthosaurus*, a big theropod quite similar to but somewhat smaller than a *T. rex.*

The Paluxy River trackway clearly shows that each time the *Pleurocoelus* moved, the stalker matched it step for step. When the herbivore turned toward the right, the *Acrocanthosaurus* did the same, purposely keeping pace and always maintaining the same distance behind its quarry. Eventually, the predator ended the stalk by breaking into a run. Within seconds it closed the gap between the two and clamped its massive jaws on the plant eater's left leg. Exactly what happened next will never be known. This is because the remainder of the trackway did not survive. Perhaps the *Pleurocoelus* managed to get away, but it is more likely that its attacker—a close cousin of *T. rex*—prevailed and departed with a full belly.

Hunter or Scavenger?

Some modern dinosaur experts have argued that the evidence of the Texas trackway is not enough by itself to prove that *T. rex* was primarily a hunter. In their view,

The T. rex had a massive, muscular body and may have been a fast runner. Its stubby forelimbs, some scientists say, were deceptively strong.

the huge theropod rarely, if ever, hunted live animals. Instead, they say, it sustained itself mainly or even exclusively by scavenging—feeding on the bodies of already dead creatures.

DID *T. REX* HAVE FEATHERS?

In the last decades of the twentieth century, paleontologists found that a number of small theropods—bipedal, carnivorous dinosaurs—had feathers. It is also now universally accepted that some of these feathered creatures survived the great extinction that occurred 65 million years ago and thereafter evolved into birds. Another fact that experts established was that the tyrannosaurids, including *T. rex*, were closely related to those much smaller feathered theropods. This quite naturally caused paleontologists to wonder if *Tyrannosaurus rex* also had feathers. Not enough direct evidence has yet been found to answer this question for sure. But theories abound. One, put forward by Xu Xing of the Chinese Academy of Sciences, suggests that baby *T. rexes* started out covered in very thin, hairlike feathers. In its juvenile years, Xing proposes, the creature steadily shed that downy covering. He and other experts point out that some species of modern elephants undergo a similar transformation. They are born with a thick covering of thin body hair—similar to feathers—that falls off before they reach adulthood.

Part of the proof cited by proponents of this theory is the fact that *T. rex* was elephant sized, and elephants are too heavy to run very fast. Top speed for an adult elephant is 10 to 15 miles per hour (16 to 24 kph)—too slow to catch several of the creatures that a large predatory dinosaur would have tried to bring down. According to a 2010 article for *National Geographic*, "The idea that *T. rex* lumbered like an elephant" fits with various studies of the dinosaur's body. One of those studies "found that *T. rex*'s leg muscles would have to have been heftier than its whole body weight for the dinosaur to have been a speed demon."[3]

Proponents of the scavenger theory also point to *T. rex*'s tiny front arms. Such small limbs and claws would have been almost useless in an attack on another dinosaur, according to this view. So *Tyrannosaurus* and other large theropods were likely not effective hunters. That left only scavenging as a means of acquiring enough food to survive.

A number of other paleontologists disagree that *T. rex* was only a scavenger, however. They say that their own studies have indicated that comparisons between modern elephants and extinct theropods can be unreliable. In this view, not only could *T. rex* run rapidly, at least for short distances, but also the creature's forelimbs were unusually strong for their size. Indeed, a study cited in a 2008 *Smithsonian* article found that "while *T. rex*'s forearms were stubby, they were buff. The muscles in the upper forearms, for instance, were 3.5 times more powerful than the same muscles in humans."[4] Thus, *Tyrannosaurus rex* clutched its prey in its small but strong forearms while tearing hunks of flesh from its unfortunate victim.

Evidence supporting both sides of the hunter-scavenger argument continues to be compelling. For that reason, most paleontologists think that both arguments are essentially correct. That is, *T. rex* often hunted living creatures. But when it had trouble finding enough prey, it resorted to scavenging already dead carcasses.

Extremely Successful

Whether eagerly killing live prey or more leisurely munching on an animal's corpse, *T. rex* was not very picky about what it ate. Evidence shows that its diet consisted of both plant- and meat-eating dinosaurs. It also consumed amphibians, small mammals, and most other creatures that inhabited North America's forests, plains, and swamps in the Late Cretaceous times.

After *T. rex* had either captured or found one of these animals and was ready to eat, the huge carnivore's two most extraordinary features went to work. One was the monstrous jaw in its 5-foot-long (1.5 m) skull. Experts

A T. rex *could consume about 500 pounds (227 kg) of meat in a single bite, thanks to its daggerlike teeth (pictured). These teeth, still attached to part of a jaw, were found with a* T. rex *skeleton in South Dakota in 1991.*

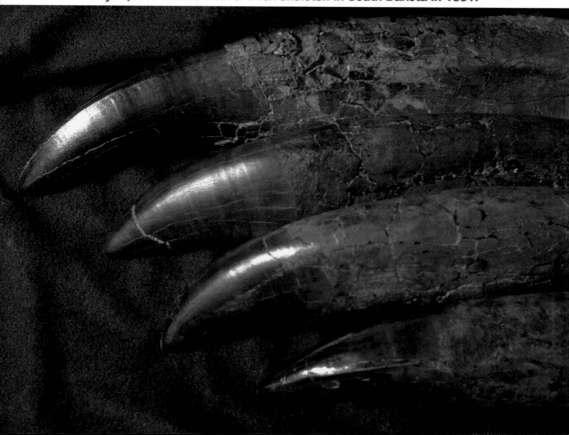

agree that this dinosaur had the most powerful, crushing bite of any land creature that has ever lived. The pressure exerted by those vice-like jaws could crush the bones of plant-eating dinosaurs as massive as four or more elephants.

The other notable attribute that helped a *Tyrannosaurus rex* feed consisted of its sixty or more daggerlike teeth. Their length varied from 6 to 12 inches (15 to 30 cm). The combination of its immensely strong jaw and the tearing ability of its teeth allowed an adult *T. rex* to consume an estimated 500 pounds (227 kg) of meat in a single bite.

That this largest tyrannosaurid usually managed to find enough food—alive or dead—can be deduced from the fact that it was extremely successful. *T. rex* survived for some 15 million years, beginning with its emergence as a species about 80 million years ago. During that era, it was the most efficient, forceful, and frightening land predator on the planet. It almost certainly would have been around much longer had it not become one of the many victims of the great mass extinction that occurred about 65 million years ago.

Chapter 2

Carcharodontosaurus

About 100 million years ago, some 30 million years before *T. rex* appeared in North America, another large, terrifying predatory dinosaur emerged on the far side of the globe. The earlier of the two monsters now bears a mouthful of a name—*Carcharodontosaurus.* It hunted in the coastal forests and wetlands that then existed across most of northern Africa, until the creature disappeared around 95 million to 93 million years ago. In the roughly 5 million to 7 million years of its existence, *Carcharodontosaurus* was one of the two or three biggest, most dangerous predators in the world.

The African *T. Rex*?

Today most of the prehistoric forests and swamps in which *Carcharodontosaurus* roamed are gone, and that sector of Africa is largely dry. Fortunately for modern science, the dryness helped preserve a number of *Carcharodontosaurus* remains, the first examples of which were found in Egypt in 1914. They consisted of part of a very large skull, some pieces of backbone and toes, a section of pelvis, and much of the rear legs. At the time, no one knew to which dinosaur these bones belonged.

A few years later, in 1927, scientist Charles Depéret and a colleague discovered some unidentified dinosaur teeth in another North African country, Algeria. At first it was not clear that the teeth belonged to the same creature whose bones had been found earlier in Egypt. But then in 1931, German paleontologist Ernst Stromer made the connection and described a new dinosaur genus he called *Carcharodontosaurus.*

All the beast's known bones were stored in a large collection of dinosaur remains in Munich, Germany, where they remained until an unexpected disaster struck. In April 1944, at the height of World War II, Allied bombers blew up the building containing the bones, obliterating them. In the decades that followed, therefore, the only proof of *Carcharodontosaurus*'s existence consisted of

Paleontologist Paul Sereno can be seen behind a model of a 5-foot-long (1.5 m) Carcharodontosaurus *skull that his team discovered in Morocco.* Carcharodontosaurus *was one of the two or three biggest and most dangerous predators in its world.*

the written notes of the scientists who had dug up the now lost bones. The situation changed again in 1995, when American paleontologist Paul Sereno found a complete skull of the great predatory dinosaur in another North African nation, Morocco. Still another full skull emerged from the ground farther south, in Nigeria, in 2006.

Experts noticed that the skulls, like the *Carcharodontosaurus* bones destroyed in the 1940s, resembled those of *Tyrannosaurus rex* in a number of ways. So over the years some scientists nicknamed the older creature the "African *T. rex.*" This name is misleading, however. On the surface, *Carcharodontosaurus* looked similar to *T. rex.* First, both were very large bipedal meat-eaters. In fact, at a length of 43 feet (13 m), an adult *Carcharodontosaurus* was slightly bigger than a grown *T. rex*, which averaged 40 feet (12 m) long. Also, both creatures had huge, muscular thighs, small forelimbs, and big jaws studded with many sharp teeth.

Yet in reality the two giant theropods were only distantly related. They lived in different eras and locales, so it would have been impossible for them to meet in the wild. In addition, the two creatures had markedly different kinds of teeth and as a result likely hunted and killed their prey in noticeably different ways.

The Shark Lizard

The issue of *Carcharodontosaurus*'s highly unusual and specialized teeth actually had a direct bearing on the choice of its long and hard-to-pronounce name (which many dinosaur buffs shorten to "Carch"). When Stromer studied the set of Carch teeth found in 1927, he noted that they were similar to and different from those of most

CARCHARODONTOSAURUS AT A GLANCE

- Scientific name: *Carcharodontosaurus saharicus*
- Scientific suborder: Theropod
- Scientific family: Carcharodontosaurid
- Range: Egypt, Morocco, and other parts of northern Africa
- Habitat: Coastal forests and wetlands
- Average size: 40 to 43 feet (12 to 13 m)
- Diet: Mainly large plant-eating dinosaurs
- Life span: Uncertain
- Key features: Muscular legs; big jaw with numerous sharp, serrated teeth
- Deadly because: Speedy and strong, with a deadly, slashing bite

other known theropods, including *T. rex*. On the *similar* side, almost all species of theropod had serrated teeth. That is, like the edge of a steak knife, the edge of each tooth bore tiny bumps and grooves that allowed it to more easily cut through thick hide and flesh.

What made Carch's teeth different from those of *T. rex* is that a typical *Tyrannosaurus* tooth, although somewhat serrated, was thick and rounded, like a banana. That gave it added strength that allowed the beast to chomp down on and crush bones as well as tear flesh. In contrast, a Carch tooth was fairly narrow, curved slightly backward, and had more pronounced serrations. This allowed the creature the highly specialized ability to slice through a prey animal's flesh much like the proverbial steak knife slashing through a thick piece of beef on a dinner plate.

Stromer also called attention to the fact that Carch's unusual teeth were extremely similar to those of a great white shark. The scientific name of that genus of shark is *Carcharodon*, from the Greek words *karcharo*, meaning "jagged," and *odonto*, meaning "teeth." To these words, Stromer added *sauros*, Greek for "lizard," and Latinized it by changing the *os* in *sauros* to *us*. (Experts traditionally render animals' scientific names in Latin.) The full name of the recently discovered dinosaur thereby became *Carcharodontosaurus*, variously translated as "great white shark lizard" or "sharp-toothed lizard."

Slash and Wait

Paleontologists point out that it was no accident that Carch and *T. rex* had different sorts of teeth, which in each case were clearly specialized for a certain task. That job had nothing to do with chewing, since evidence shows that large theropods swallowed hunks of meat whole, rather than chewing them. Instead, tooth specialization in these creatures reflected the manner in which they hunted and killed prey. *T. rex*, most experts believe, first stalked and then attacked and captured a victim. Then the huge predator used its small but strong forelimbs to hold the prey while it began tearing apart and eating the still-struggling animal. Evolving in a different time and place, *Carcharodontosaurus* developed its own remarkable hunting strategy. Some modern experts have called this technique "slash and wait." Clearly, it required considerably less effort and energy than the more active hunting tactics employed by *T. rex* and many other large predatory dinosaurs.

The narrow, curved tooth of a Carcharodontosaurus *reveals a serrated edge. The shape and structure of its teeth enabled the* Carcharodontosaurus *to effortlessly slice through flesh.*

First, like other predators through the ages, a Carch stalked its prey. In one likely scenario, it found a herd of large herbivores, its principal food source, and immediately searched for the weakest link. That might have been an animal that was sick or injured, or perhaps one that was just too slow to keep up with its mates. Using classic stalking methods, from a distance the Carch matched its victim's movements almost step for step.

Then, when it felt the time was right, the *Carcharodontosaurus* leapt forward and in a few swift bounds approached the straggler from behind. At this point, the Carch's specialized teeth did their awful work. In Cavan Scott's words, the big hunter delivered a "devastating bite to its prey, its serrated teeth slashing deep into the flesh, causing massive trauma."[5]

At this point in such an attack, a *T. rex* would have held on and tried to start feeding. But quite different instincts drove the Carch. It suddenly let go of the severely wounded prey, stepped back, and for as long as it took waited for the moaning, limping beast to collapse. Perhaps this took only ten or fifteen minutes. Or it might sometimes have been an hour or two or more. However long it took, Scott says, the Carch did not "waste energy chasing the wounded creature. It just [stood] patiently, waiting for the inevitable."[6] Indeed, the prey's fate had been fully sealed earlier, in the few seconds it had taken the Carch's huge serrated teeth to deliver the death blow. When the victim finally fell, never again to arise, the triumphant theropod leisurely walked over and began eating.

Its Considerable Energies

Why it was so important for *Carcharodontosaurus* to save as much energy as possible during its hunts does not have a definitive explanation, but paleontologists have ventured some educated guesses. One often-cited reason is competition from other large meat eaters. In North America in the Late Cretaceous period, *T. rex* in a very real sense reigned supreme. No other predator was big enough and ferocious enough to mess with it, so it could afford to expend as much energy as it wanted when hunting.

By contrast, earlier, in Middle Cretaceous times, Carch shared the forests and plains of northern Africa with the enormous and dangerous *Spinosaurus*. Individuals of the two genuses probably encountered each other from time to time and almost certainly viewed each other as enemies. No evidence suggests that *Spinosaurus* actually hunted *Carcharodontosaurus*. But these beasts may well have occasionally clashed over which had the right to scavenge a meal from a large herbivore's corpse. It

A MIDDLE CRETACEOUS BATTLE

No evidence for fights between *Carcharodontosaurus* and another large African predator, *Spinosaurus*, has yet been found. But some paleontologists and other dinosaur buffs have speculated on what such a matchup might have been like. Here, researcher Joe Smith uses accurate information about these creatures to re-create a Middle Cretaceous battle between a male *Carcharodontosaurus* and a female *Spinosaurus*.

She roars, and turning, clamps down on the *Carcharodontosaur*'s back. He roars in anger, and twists around, swatting the *Spinosaur* with his tail. She stumbles back [and] is blindsided [and] thrown back down. [Rising], she briefly stands on only her back legs, and swings her arm at the *Carcharodontosaurus*. He bellows in pain, and bites down on the *Spinosaur*'s hand. Shaking and twisting, he rips it clean off. The *Spinosaur* howls and screams, as blood erupts from the wound. She charges into the *Carcharodontosaurus*, pushing him backwards, then hits him with her tail. Almost losing his balance he is caught off guard [but then] clamps down on her neck, with a bone shattering bite, and she screams in pain, but goes down. [After] hitting the ground, she lays still. The *Carcharodontosaurus* roars in triumph, setting his foot down on the dead predator.

Joe Smith, "Prehistoric Arena—Battle Three: *Carcharodontosaurus* vs. *Spinosaurus*," *CurryMan21's Blog*, Dinosaur Home, 2015. www.dinosaur home.com.

may be, therefore, that Carch tried to conserve as much energy as possible so as to be ready to defend itself against a rival predator if the need suddenly arose.

Moreover, some experts have proposed that *Spinosaurus* was only one of Carch's regular challengers. No less threatening, in this view, were other Carches. Some evidence strongly suggests that juvenile or adult Carches, or perhaps both, sometimes grappled with

A Carcharodontosaurus *guards its kill against a small but determined rival. Although it might not have used a lot of energy to kill its prey,* Carcharodontosaurus *would have vigorously defended its catch if another dinosaur lurked nearby.*

and wounded one another. Paleontologists have advanced several theories to explain the causes of such inter-genus rivalry. One suggestion for why one *Carcharodontosaurus* might have opposed another is that they skirmished over food. If a juvenile or adult Carch brought down and began eating a prey animal and another Carch appeared and tried to steal the meal, a fight would almost certainly have ensued. In another scenario, juvenile Carches may well have engaged in play fighting. The goal was constructive—to allow the creatures to practice certain skills they would need later in life. But at times such play likely got too rough. Some paleontologists point out that lions and other large modern predators have frequently been observed engaging in similar behavior.

Still another possible outlet for a Carch's aggressive tendencies was overly forceful courtship rituals. For instance, scientists have observed that when members of some reptile and bird species mate, the male bites the female's nose and holds on to her until the deed is finished. Thus, *Carcharodontosaurus* may have divided its considerable energies among several vigorous activities, of which hunting was only one.

Perhaps it was this flexibility that made Carch so successful. Indeed, as a genus it might have lasted much longer than the 5 million to 7 million years in which it was a leading African predator. Ultimately, however, changes in local coastlines and landforms steadily did it in. Between about 95 million and 93 million years ago, sea levels dropped, and the extensive moist habitat in which *Carcharodontosaurus* hunted dried up. The majestic creature evidently could not adapt quickly enough to these changes, and in the proverbial blink of an eye within the immensely long span of geologic time, it was gone.

Chapter 3

Spinosaurus

Paleontologists have determined that the mighty theropod *Carcharodontosaurus* shared the well-watered region of Middle Cretaceous North Africa with an even larger meat-eating dinosaur called *Spinosaurus.* The exact period in which *Spinosaurus* flourished is a bit uncertain. Estimates run from as early as 112 million years ago to as late as 93 million years ago. *Carcharodontosaurus* thrived between 100 million and 93 million years ago. For at least a few million years, therefore, the two were arch rivals and competitors occupying the apex, or top, of North Africa's food chain.

Another thing the two beasts had in common was the formal Latin names that modern experts assigned them. The bigger creature's scientific name is *Spinosaurus aegyptiacus.* The first of these words is Latin for "spine lizard," a reference to the large, sail-like bulge on its back. The other word, *aegyptiacus*, is Latin for "Egyptian," based on the fact that the first remains of the monster were discovered in Egypt. Thus, its scientific name means "Egyptian spine lizard."

A Life in the Water

Spinosaurus was the largest known carnivorous dinosaur. Not enough of its bones have yet been unearthed to establish how big an adult of this genus could grow. But experts feel confident enough to estimate an average length of at least 50 feet (15 m) and a weight of 8 to 9 tons (7 to 8 metric tons). That means that a large *Spinosaurus* would have dwarfed an average-size *T. rex*, the famous and fearsome apex predator of Cretaceous North America.

It was not simply *Spinosaurus*'s great size that made it frightening and deadly, however. It was also highly versatile, or flexible and adaptive, as a hunter—more so than either *T. rex* or *Carcharodontosaurus.* The latter two dinosaurs were strictly land predators. So if an animal that one of them was chasing fled into a river or lake, the attacker likely gave up the chase.

In stark contrast, *Spinosaurus* could and did hunt both on land and in the water. In fact, it is currently the only known partly aquatic dinosaur. Noted University of Chicago paleontologist Nizar Ibrahim, who has studied *Spinosaurus* remains in detail, states, "When we look at the body proportions, the animal was clearly not as agile on land as other dinosaurs were, so I think it spent a substantial amount of time in the water." Moreover, the creature's "proportions were really bizarre. The hind limbs were shorter than in other predatory dinosaurs, the foot claws were quite wide, and the feet almost paddle shaped. We thought: 'Wow! This looks like adaptations for a life mainly spent in water.'"[7]

Ibrahim also noticed that *Spinosaurus* exhibited other traits usually associated with aquatic animals. "The snout," he said, "is very similar to that of fish-eating crocodiles, with interlocking cone-shaped teeth. And even the bones look more like those of aquatic animals than of other dinosaurs. They are very dense and that is something you see in animals like penguins or sea cows, and that is important for buoyancy in the water." Ibrahim's overall impression of *Spinosaurus* is that "it is a really bizarre dinosaur! There's no real blueprint for it."[8]

Hunting Strategies: Land

Thus, *Spinosaurus* was able to hunt in the water as well as on land. Ibrahim and other scientists think that it did not venture too far from riverbanks, lakes, and estuaries. In part this was because of its huge size. Too bulky and awkward to run very fast and far, when hunting on land it likely employed stealth whenever possible.

Dinosaurs, which were almost exclusively land creatures, had to drink water to stay alive. So a typical pond or riverbank almost certainly attracted at least some dinosaurs of various species at different times of the day. Probably they tried to drink their fill and leave quickly because they could sense that such an area was not safe.

In this they were correct, because *Spinosaurus* was frequently lurking nearby, waiting for its chance to strike. One likely land-hunting strategy the great carnivore used was to hide in the lush greenery that thrived near the shore. When it saw a lone individual drinking, particularly if it was lame or wounded, the *Spinosaurus* suddenly leapt forward and in perhaps no more than two or three bounds captured the victim's tail or leg in its crocodile-like jaws. The big predator's next move, experts surmise, was to drag the stunned and terrified prey into the water and drown it. In a similar manner, modern crocodiles and alligators routinely drag land animals into the water and drown them.

The claw of a Spinosaurus (pictured) suggests a wide, almost paddle-shaped foot. This shape would have helped the semiaquatic dinosaur make its way through water.

Spinosaurus probably utilized a second hunting strategy designed to capture land creatures attempting to drink from a river or other water source. Very adapted to the water, the monstrous predator lay down in shallow water, leaving only its nostrils, needed for breathing, above the surface. It could have lain on its side to keep its spinal sail from protruding upward and giving its presence away. When a potential prey ventured too close to the concealed *Spinosaurus* and lowered its head to drink, the enormous predator abruptly used it massive tail and muscular forelimbs to push itself upward and forward. In mere seconds, the startled drinker was dragged away to a horrifying death.

Hunting Strategies: Water

Spinosaurus's hunting strategy for killing aquatic creatures was quite different. Here again, it may have employed two different approaches. One was to stand very still in shallow or moderately deep water and wait for large fish to swim by. Then, as modern herons do, the big hunter suddenly lowered its mouth and yanked

A Spinosaurus stands very still in shallow water as it waits for unwitting prey. With its powerful crocodile-like jaws, it could quickly snap up a fish or other animal.

SPINOSAURUS AT A GLANCE

- **Scientific name:** *Spinosaurus aegyptiacus*
- **Scientific suborder: Theropod**
- **Scientific family: Spinosaurid**
- **Range: Northern Africa**
- **Habitat: Wetlands, swamps, and riverbanks**
- **Average size: 50 feet (15 m) or more**
- **Diet: Fish, birds, small dinosaurs**
- **Life span: Unknown**
- **Key features: Huge body, sail-like hump on its back, crocodile-like snout**
- **Deadly because: Big, powerful; able to swim or walk on land**

the prey up and out of the water. *Spinosaurus* likely swallowed the smaller catches whole. But in the case of larger prey, as Cavan Scott writes, the hunter threw "the bucking fish onto the bank, stamping on it with a giant foot to keep it still. Powerful claws slashed into the [fish's] skin, killing [it] and carving up the fishy flesh."[9]

Another water-based strategy that *Spinosaurus* may have used to hunt its next meal relied on this dinosaur's unique ability to swim. Most experts are convinced that it was a strong swimmer with a taste for sharks. "*Spinosaurus* pursued sharks and other large fish in the deep river system it inhabited,"[10] one researcher states. The giant theropod was able to move swiftly through the

EVIDENCE THAT SPINOSAURUS COULD SWIM

In a landmark 2014 scientific paper published in the distinguished journal *Science*, a team of paleontologists headed by Dr. Nizar Ibrahim reported that the huge theropod dinosaur *Spinosaurus* was a skilled and avid swimmer. These experts based their findings on remains of the creature found across North Africa over the course of decades. It was the only known dinosaur that could hunt in the water as well as on land, they say. One piece of evidence they cite is that *Spinosaurus* had wide, flat, paddle-like feet and a tail equipped with very loose, flexible joints. Both of these features were designed to allow the beast to propel itself through an underwater environment. Also, the carnivorous monster's nostrils were located on top, rather than at the front, of its head. That unusual arrangement made it possible for *Spinosaurus* to partially submerge and breathe intermittently as it swam. In addition, the researchers found hundreds of tiny openings within the bones at the tip of its snout. Almost identical to a feature found in modern crocodiles and alligators, these made the semiaquatic dinosaur extremely sensitive to pressure waves generated in the water by the movement of fish and other prey.

water, thanks in part to the loosely connected bones in its tail. These made it possible for the tail to bend in a wavelike manner. In turn, that action gave the creature a powerful push forward, quite similar to how some species of bony fish propel themselves through the water.

Such skillful aquatic behavior is extraordinary not only because all other known dinosaurs hunted strictly on land, but also because of where *Spinosaurus* seems to have been headed as a genus. Had it not died out because of rapid loss of habitat between 95 million and 93 million years ago, it might have steadily evolved into a solely marine creature. Biologists have observed this same scenario in nature in several other cases, including that of whales, which developed from land animals.

"An Alien from Outer Space"

Some paleontologists have suggested that another of *Spinosaurus*'s unusual features—the large sail resting along its back—could be seen sticking up above the

Bony spines, visible in this Spinosaurus *skeleton, supported the dinosaur's spinal sail. One theory about the sail's purpose is that it made the* Spinosaurus *look bigger and more menacing to other dinosaurs.*

water's surface as the creature swam. This impressive growth was supported by a number of bony spines. The longest were almost 7 feet (2 m) long, and all may have been connected by a layer of weblike tissue.

Experts still debate the uses for this odd physical feature. One possibility is that it was involved in mating rituals, since it might have been a way for males to attract females or vice versa. Another theory proposes that the sail was nature's attempt to scare away large, threatening predators, like *Carcharodontosaurus.* Many dinosaurs seem to have had substandard vision. So from a distance the sail would have appeared to them to be a solid extension of *Spinosaurus*'s body; in other words, they saw that dinosaur as even bigger than it really was, making them think twice about tangling with it.

Still another way that *Spinosaurus* may have employed the spines on its back was as a kind of heat regulator. In this respect, a few paleontologists have suggested that the spines were not part of a thin sail, but the bony support for a big hump similar to the kind seen in modern bison. On days when the hot sun beat down on the creature for long periods, the hump would have acted as a shield against that warmth, providing some relief. At the same time, fat stored inside the hump would have supplied extra energy for when the animal required it.

Thus, *Spinosaurus* was not simply a huge, frightening, and deadly predator. It also possessed an exceptional combination of unusual, quirky traits that made it one of the oddest creatures that ever walked the planet. In an interview for *National Geographic*, Ibrahim colorfully but aptly remarked, "Working on this animal was like studying an alien from outer space. It's unlike any other dinosaur I have ever seen."[11]

Chapter 4

Troodon

Well after *Spinosaurus* and its fellow large theropod *Carcharodontosaurus* went extinct in Africa, the mighty *T. rex* enjoyed the rank of apex predator in North America. Yet *Tyrannosaurus* was not the only deadly and successful Late Cretaceous hunter in the areas that would later become Canada and the United States. Another was *Troodon*, which means "wounding tooth."

Although *Troodon* was a theropod that walked on two legs like the other three, it was physically very different from them in other ways. First, it was far smaller in stature. *Troodons* that dwelled in the area that is now Alberta, Canada, and further south were roughly 8 feet (2.4 m) long from the tip of the snout to the end of the tail and weighed about 110 pounds (50 kg). Experts think that members of this genus that lived farther north were about twice as long and twice as heavy as their more southerly cousins.

At first glance, it may seem surprising that such a small creature can be ranked as a predator no less deadly than *T. rex* and the other monstrous giants. But that is where *Troodon*'s most crucial difference with the others lies. Although the huge predators in question were immensely strong and possessed enormous jaws filled with sharp teeth, they were not very bright. In fact, they had just enough brainpower to walk, hunt for their next meal, and survive long enough to reproduce.

In stunning contrast, it appears that *Troodon* was the smartest of all the dinosaurs. In fact, many paleontologists speculate that it was intelligent enough to understand cooperative behavior among members of its own kind. Some evidence suggests that such teamwork extended to hunting in packs. Clearly, despite the small size of a single *Troodon*, seven, ten, or more vicious, hungry *Troodons* working together could have brought down even the largest plant-eating dinosaur.

Unusually Large Brains

Paleontologists have a limited amount of evidence to work with in their efforts to determine the intelligence of *Troodon*. Only a few remains of this fascinating dinosaur have been found so far. The first such artifact was a single tooth unearthed in Montana in 1856 by American scientist Joseph Leidy. He thought it belonged to an ancient but fairly ordinary lizard, and not until 1901 did other experts conclude the tooth had once belonged to a dinosaur.

Other remains of the creature came to light during the twentieth century, including pieces of claws, feet, and tails. They were discovered in Texas, New Mexico, Canada, and Alaska. For several decades, many of these fossils were thought to have been those of a small, birdlike dinosaur called *Stenonychosaurus*. But by the first decade of the twenty-first century, most dinosaur experts had concluded that they were not dealing with a new species. Instead, the bones actually belonged to juvenile members of a species of *Troodon*.

Troodons—*small, agile, and fast—may have hunted in packs (pictured).
Cooperative behavior of this sort is associated with greater intelligence.*

However, Cavan Scott points out, "while experts
might disagree about names and species, they all agree
that *Troodon* was an intelligent dinosaur."[12] Indeed,
when skulls of the beast were first found and examined,
it became clear that they had once housed unusually
large brains. That is, those brains were uncommonly big
compared to the brains of other dinosaurs.

To figure out the relative intelligence of a dinosaur—or
any animal, for that matter—scientists often use a formula
called encephalization quotient, or EQ. In simple terms, it
compares the weight of a creature's brain to the weight of
its body. In theory, if two animals are equal in weight but
one has a brain twice the size of the other, the one with

- Scientific name: *Troodon formosus*
- Scientific suborder: Theropod
- Scientific family: Troodontid
- Range: Northern America
- Habitat: Upland woodlands
- Average size: 8 to 13 feet (2.5 to 4 m) long
- Diet: Plants, small reptiles and mammals; also large herbivorous dinosaurs
- Life span: Uncertain; reached adulthood in three to five years
- Key features: Small, sharp teeth; sickle-shaped claw on second toe; large forward-looking eyes
- Deadly because: Unusually intelligent, fast runner; probably a pack hunter

the bigger brain is twice as smart. Using this system, experts have ranked *Troodon* as by far the brainiest known dinosaur. Generally speaking, an adult of the genus was about eight times smarter than the herbivores it hunted and around four times smarter than a grown *T. rex*.

The Benefits of Cooperation

Here, the word *hunted* is key because hunting was the activity in which *Troodon*'s high intelligence most showed itself and affected the creature's life and survival. It was a theropod, and all theropods hunted to obtain at least some of their food. As near as scientists can tell, large theropods like *T. rex* hunted singly. This was likely because such a beast lacked enough intelligence to realize that there was a lot to be gained through cooperation with others of its kind.

In contrast, paleontologists speculate that *Troodon* possessed sufficient intelligence to recognize the benefits of cooperative hunting, more often called pack hunting. It is seen today in large predatory mammals such as wild dogs, wolves, lions, and hyenas. Clearly, pack hunting, which requires a certain amount of social organization among members of a species, significantly increases the chances of that group's success and survival.

A computer illustration comparing dinosaur brain sizes reveals the relatively large brain of a Troodon *(bottom) and a much smaller brain of a common long-necked dinosaur known as* Camarasus. Troodon *is considered the smartest of the dinosaurs.*

The success of a pack of *Troodons* in search of food was enhanced by a number of physical factors. First, because a typical *Troodon* was smaller than an average adult human and had muscular, ostrichlike legs, it was almost certainly fast and agile. No one knows how fast it could run. But most experts say it was probably comparable to the top speed of a modern ostrich—about 45 miles per hour (72 kph). That is close to four times quicker than a world-class human sprinter and without doubt far faster than any of the large plant-eating dinosaurs could move.

Another superior and important physical trait *Troodon* possessed was front-facing eyes, giving it binocular vision (in which the fields of view overlap) and depth perception (the ability to see in three dimensions). Most dinosaurs' eyes faced outward in different directions, which meant that they *lacked* depth perception. In turn, that limited their ability to determine the position and distance of objects, including nearby animals. Having depth perception, *Troodon* was able to target, jump at, and bite its prey with considerable accuracy, making it a skilled and successful hunter.

Added to its impressive speed and excellent vision, *Troodon*'s high intelligence allowed it to apply those qualities specifically to pack hunting. A group of these hunters likely targeted a large plant-eating dinosaur whenever possible. This is because there had to be enough meat to feed all the attackers, plus their babies, if any.

Pack Hunting: Methods and Stalking

A number of scientists have tried to reconstruct how *Troodon* and other closely related small theropods pack

TROODON'S POSSIBLE DESCENDANTS

Paleontologist Dale Russell of North Carolina State University is among a number of dinosaur experts who marvel at *Troodon's* high degree of intelligence. This trait not only gave the creature the drive to hunt in packs, experts contend, but likely motivated further increases in intelligence level. Russell thinks that if most dinosaurs had not gone extinct 65 million years ago, *Troodon* might well have become progressively smarter and followed an evolutionary path similar to the one humanity's primate ancestors did. In the 1980s the paleontologist constructed a life-size model of the possible end product of such theoretical dinosaurian evolution. Dubbed the "Dinosauroid" by Russell, the model still rests in the Canadian Museum of Nature in Ottawa. Standing upright on two legs like a human being, *Troodon's* hypothetical descendant possesses three-fingered hands with opposable thumbs, a trait crucial to tool use and building a technological civilization. Russell's thought-provoking creation is widely viewed as a reminder of how blind chance can drive natural events in dramatic new directions. Humanity itself is the fortunate product of such a chance event, Russell says. Had the dinosaurs not gone extinct when they did, he continues, modern civilization may have been fashioned by three-fingered reptilian hands.

hunted. The starting point for such speculations is usually to observe how modern predators of similar size accomplish such attacks. "The aim of a predator is to kill its prey without being killed or injured itself," Bloomsburg

University paleontologist Alan D. Gishlick points out. Attacks by lions, hyenas, and other pack hunters, he says, "are directed either to the rear or side of the prey."[13]

In addition to the direction of such an attack, experts consider the actual method the pack of hunters employ. Such techniques can be classified under names such as lurk and wait, stalk and pounce, attack with jaws, and attack with claws, Gishlick explains. Often the pack hunters combine biting with clawing in various ways. He continues, "In some pack hunting, multiple predators bite the extremities of the prey and hang on until the prey is dragged down. Predators that use the claw attack lead with the forelimbs and use the jaws to deliver a killing blow."[14]

Using such methods, a pack of Troodons could conceivably have overpowered, injured, and killed a fairly large plant-eating dinosaur. One such creature that experts have frequently proposed as probable prey for packs of Troodons is Maiasaura, the so-called good mother reptile. An adult was an imposing animal measuring about 30 feet (9 m) long and weighing some 2.5 tons (2.3 metric tons). A single hungry Troodon would probably not have tried to tangle with it. Instead, it would have raided the Maiasaura's nest and stolen an egg or recently hatched baby.

However, a pack of Troodons that was out to find larger amounts of fresh meat would have stalked any juvenile or even full-grown Maiasaura that strayed from its herd. As one modern researcher envisions it, the larger dinosaur may have "stopped for a moment, nostrils flaring, eyes dilating in fear." It almost certainly could smell its stalkers, which were hiding nearby. These odors were familiar because in the past it had detected them "in the dead of night, nights in which it woke up in the nest to find fewer eggs than there were before." The *Maiasaura* seemed able to sense hints "of fresh blood, of intelligence, of predatory instinct, of death. All this it smelled, and it was terrified."[15]

Pack Hunting: Attacking and Killing

When they judged it to be the right moment, the *Troodons* would have sprung from their hiding places and launched the attack. Darting to and fro far faster than the lumbering *Maiasaura* could react, they would have struck at its hind legs and tail, wounding it. One or

A hungry Troodon *raids the nest of another dinosaur. When hunting in packs,* Troodons *probably searched for larger prey, but eggs and hatchlings offered an easy meal whenever they hunted alone.*

more of the smaller beasts might well have leapt onto its back and bitten at its neck.

The stricken *Maiasaura* lacked the speed, sharp teeth, and sicklelike claws of its attackers, so it used the only effective weapon it had—its massive tail. In fact, a well-aimed swipe of that fleshy appendage would likely have knocked a *Troodon* unconscious or even injured it badly. Perhaps the larger creature was fortunate enough to eliminate one or two of its foe in this manner. But even so, there were more than enough *Troodons* remaining to continue the assault. African wild dogs hunt in packs of six to twenty or more members, and small theropods probably did the same.

As a number of modern pack hunters do, the *Troodons* probably bit and slashed at their prey incessantly for a few minutes but then backed away a bit. Thinking it had a chance to escape, the *Maiasaura* would have mustered whatever energy it could and run for it. But its frenzied staggering only caused more blood to pour from its wounds and further exhausted it. The more intelligent attackers allowed their prey to grow weaker like this for a few minutes or more and then renewed the onslaught.

Eventually, the "good mother" dinosaur was unable to go on and collapsed. One or more *Troodons* then slashed open its throat to finish it off. Zoologists have documented that a pack of hyenas can consume a dead zebra completely, bones and all, in an hour. A full-grown *Maiasaura* was much bigger than a zebra. Yet even if it took them several hours, the *Troodons* would have polished off their entire kill, very likely taking some of the meat back to their young. Merciless, bloody scenes like this one occurred as a matter of course in prehistoric North America, demonstrating how deceptively deadly even small predatory dinosaurs could be.

Chapter 5

Sinornithosaurus

During the past few decades, scientists uncovered a large body of evidence indicating that modern birds evolved directly from a small group of theropod dinosaurs. These creatures, which were cousins of *Troodon*, typically had certain birdlike traits in common. These included lightweight skeletons with long, mostly slender legs; excellent vision, often with front-facing eyes; bodies covered partially or totally with feathers; and in some cases forelimbs that were on their way to developing into wings. Over the course of about 50 million years, these creatures did become early birds, which constituted the only dinosaurian group that escaped the mass extinction 65 million years ago.

One of the most fascinating of these bird ancestors was first discovered in 1999 in Liaoning Province in China. Chinese paleontologist Xu Xing and some colleagues found an almost complete skeleton of the creature, which they named *Sinornithosaurus millenii*. The name means "Chinese bird-lizard of the new millennium." With a length of about 4 feet (1.2 m) and a weight of 7 pounds (3 kg), it was only about the size of a turkey, which is small for a dinosaur. Xing and the others determined that *Sinornithosaurus* lived in the vast, deep forests that covered much of what is now China between 125 million and 122 million years ago, in the Early Cretaceous period.

At first glance, it might seem unusual that an animal as small as *Sinornithosaurus* could be dangerous or deadly. It certainly posed no threat to larger dinosaurs like the giant herbivores and big carnivorous hunters like

The fossilized remains of a juvenile Sinornithosaurus *(pictured) were discovered in 1999 in China. Though small by dinosaur standards,* Sinornithosaurus *represented a real threat to animals such as rodents, lizards, and frogs.*

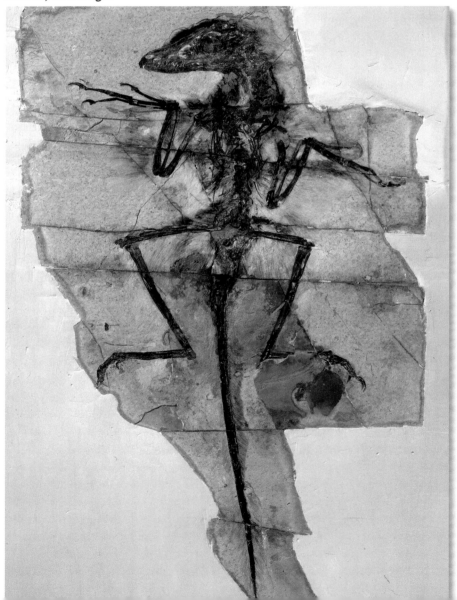

T. rex. Yet in nature, everything is relative to the specific surroundings in which a creature lives. Although large plant and meat eaters paid little or no attention to small rodents, lizards, frogs, and the many tiny dinosaurs that populated the typical forest floor, those small animals were far from safe. Even on the miniature scale of their daily lives, there were deadly predators that hunted them, and *Sinornithosaurus* was one of the most effective of those hunters.

Flying Versus Gliding

The fact that this Early Cretaceous predator had feathers and wings naturally raises the question of whether it could fly. Flying animals have always possessed certain survival advantages over many that cannot fly. But early on, Xing and his colleagues calculated that despite its feathers and wings, *Sinornithosaurus* was technically not a bird and lacked the ability to fly. They suggested that the feathers had not initially developed for flight. Instead, the creature probably employed its feathers to help stay camouflaged and hidden in the underbrush while stalking its prey. Also, feathers might have been used for display—that is, for showing off in hopes of attracting mates.

In addition, feathers would have aided in insulating small dinosaurs from cold night temperatures. Small theropods were very active creatures, which would have caused a lot of their natural body heat to escape each day. In contrast, larger dinosaurs—much like today's rhinos and elephants—had sufficient body mass to hold plenty of heat in. But because small dinosaurs like *Sinornithosaurus* lacked that extra body mass, they required some other sort of insulation, and feathers filled the bill.

- Scientific name: *Sinornithosaurus millenii*
- Scientific suborder: Theropod
- Scientific family: Dromaeosaurid
- Range: Northern China
- Habitat: Forests
- Average size: 4 feet (1.2 m) long; about 7 pounds (3 kg)
- Diet: Small dinosaurs, lizards, frogs, rodents
- Life span: Unknown
- Key features: Feathers, wings, forward-facing eyes
- Deadly because: Fast runner, possibly venomous, able to glide

Still, some scientists say, *Sinornithosaurus*'s wings and feathers *could* have given it one very effective advantage in hunting. Namely, they might have made it easier for a member of the species to leap through tree branches when chasing a prospective meal. The wings also may have allowed the creature to glide downward from a high branch to the ground. In these activities, one researcher suggests, "its rigid tail acted as a counterbalance, allowing pinpoint accuracy and freeing the powerful feet-claws."[16]

For example, picture a *Sinornithosaurus* perched on a tree branch high above the forest floor. It waits patiently for a small rodent-like mammal to crawl from a burrow. With its keen eyesight, the feathered predator sees the prey emerge and when the moment is right leaps outward into the air. Like a modern flying squirrel (which also cannot actually fly), it glides silently downward and lands directly on the prey. At the same time, it grabs the mammal in its sharp feet-claws and within seconds bites into the captured creature and starts feeding.

A Poisonous Bite?

Yet even if *Sinornithosaurus* was indeed capable of leaping through the treetops and gliding to the ground, neither of these may have been its deadliest attribute. In 2009 a group of scientists led by Chinese geologist Enpu Gong studied a well-preserved skull of that dinosaur. They immediately noticed that some of the teeth in the jaw's midsection had grooves on their outer surfaces. One surprised team member exclaimed, "Wow, that's a venomous animal!"[17] The team not only speculated that the teeth grooves delivered venom, but they also suggested that a small hollow area in the jawbone just above those teeth was where the sack containing the deadly toxin once lay.

Gong and the others therefore conjectured that when attacking prey, *Sinornithosaurus* may have bitten the other animals and injected venom much as modern snakes do. In the months that followed, a number of researchers and expert observers devised possible hunting and attack scenarios based on this theory. In one, a male *Sinornithosaurus* and its mate are ambushed by two *Buitreraptors*. (*Buitreraptor* was a theropod similar to but slightly larger than *Sinornithosaurus*.) The reconstruction takes place beside and around a *Sinornithosaurus* nest containing eggs.

Although Sinornithosaurus *(pictured) had birdlike features and primitive feathers, it could not fly. The feathers probably helped* Sinornithosaurus *hide in the underbrush while stalking prey.*

That *Sinornithosaurus* reproduced by laying eggs is almost certain. Indeed, paleontologists believe that all theropod dinosaurs, the ancestors of birds, laid eggs in nests just as birds do. Although *Sinornithosaurus* could climb trees and probably did so when hunting, it could not fly. So it did not nest in trees as birds do, but rather made its nests on the ground, likely in moist earth. Since such a nest was open to attack by predators, one or both of the parents had to guard the eggs at all times.

A Secret Weapon

Thus, the reconstruction begins with the two *Sinornithosauruses* guarding their nest. Suddenly, the two *Buitreraptors* appear from the nearby underbrush and go for the eggs. The female *Sinornithosaurus* hisses and screeches to scare off the attackers, but they keep coming. As she pecks at them with her teeth bared, they dodge and weave, trying to avoid her deadly bite.

Her mate also enters the fray. He starts to grapple with the smaller *Buitreraptor* while she fights the larger one, which while lunging for an egg makes a fatal mistake. The creature gets too close to the female *Sinornithosaurus*'s dangerous mouth. "With her long fangs," the reconstruction states, "she clamps down on his shoulder. As he screeches in pain, she pushes him off."[18]

At first, the bitten attacker has yet to feel the poison's effects, so it keeps coming and manages to grab an egg from the nest. But mere seconds later, "the venom takes effect and he stumbles, dropping the egg," and "as he lays on the ground, his limbs lose mobility and he begins to die."[19] Seeing this, the other *Buitreraptor* turns and runs back into the forest. In this scenario, the *Sinornithosauruses* win the battle and save their eggs largely due to their secret weapon—a venomous bite.

Not long after Gong and his associates introduced the theory that *Sinornithosaurus* delivered venom to its prey and enemies, that idea ignited a scientific debate. In 2010 another team of experts expressed doubt that the small dinosaur hunted or fought this way. Those scientists pointed out that several other species of theropod had similar grooves in their teeth, so *Sinornithosaurus* was not unique in that way. The debate has continued, and paleontologists remain divided on the issue. At the

FROM THE TREES DOWN

Paleontologists have confirmed that small theropods like *Sinornithosaurus* were the direct ancestors of birds. Although that particular dinosaur could not fly, it had most of the physical attributes that would allow some of its descendants to fly. Among these were feathers, lightweight bones, and winglike forelimbs. In addition, *Sinornithosaurus* demonstrated hunting-related behaviors consistent with one of the leading theories for how the first birds learned to fly. Its technical name is the arboreal theory. But it is better known by its nickname—"from the trees down." It contends that *Sinornithosaurus* and some other small theropods sometimes climbed trees in order to capture small animals that dwelled in the forest canopy. Once those small dinosaurs made it into the tree branches, they faced the very real danger of falling. In order to avoid injury or death, they may have instinctively used their outstretched feathered forelimbs to help them glide to the ground. The arboreal theory suggests that over time their forearms and feathers increasingly adapted to this behavior, becoming true wings. Moreover, properly flapping those wings while gliding eventually led to true flight.

same time, some of them have proposed an interesting compromise. It could be, they say, that *Sinornithosaurus* was indeed venomous, and so were *all* the small carnivorous dinosaurs that had the telltale grooves in their teeth.

Monsters of the Food Chain

Whether these various small bipedal dinosaurs had venomous bites, there is no doubt that they often competed with one another for the same prey. For example, all the several species of small theropods that inhabited China in the Early Cretaceous period, including *Sinornithosaurus*, were carnivorous. So they all went after dinosaur eggs, as well as small rodent-like mammals, turtles, lizards, and other relatively small animals.

In addition, there is overwhelming evidence that those other animals included fellow small theropods. One of the most striking proofs for this savage reality was discovered in 2012 in China by paleontologists from Canada's

Some scientists believe that Sinornithosaurus *fangs (pictured in fossilized form) held a nasty surprise: deadly venom that gave this small dinosaur an advantage over other creatures.*

University of Alberta. The find included the well-preserved remains of a *Sinocalliopteryx*, an Early Cretaceous theropod measuring about 8 feet (2.4 m) long and weighing about 40 pounds (18 kg). In the creature's stomach were the bones of three smaller dinosaurs that the *Sinocalliopteryx* had eaten shortly before its death. "The fact that this *Sinocalliopteryx* had not one but three undigested [bird-like dinosaurs] in its stomach indicates it was a voracious eater and a very active hunter,"[20] commented Scott Persons, who assisted the University of Alberta scientists.

One of those three tiny theropods that had the misfortune of being the bigger theropod's lunch was none other than a *Sinornithosaurus*. This clearly shows nature's food chain in all its stark but endlessly efficient operation. As remains true today, back in the age of dinosaurs the largest animals ate smaller ones, which in turn consumed still smaller ones.

In Early Cretaceous times in China, *Sinornithosaurus* appears to have rested roughly in the middle of the local food chain. Beneath it in that chain were the creatures it ate, including rodents, frogs, and smaller dinosaurs. Those smaller animals in turn feasted on still tinier prey, such as snails, worms, and insects.

Meanwhile, above *Sinornithosaurus* in the food chain were bigger theropods like *Sinocalliopteryx*. Moreover, that fierce hunter was itself stalked and eaten by a still larger predatory theropod, *Yangchuanosaurus*. (Similar to but somewhat smaller than *T. rex*, *Yangchuanosaurus* occupied the apex of China's food chain in that era.) Thus, although *Sinornithosaurus* was without doubt a deadly predator, it remained always in danger of becoming a meal for one of the other lethal monsters that inhabited its world.

Chapter 6

Predator X

Despite the best efforts of scientists and educators, a number of myths and misconceptions about dinosaurs still exist. For example, many people continue to assume that all dinosaurs were enormous brutes like *T. rex* and the giant plant eaters it hunted. The existence of *Troodon*, *Sinornithosaurus*, and other dinosaurs smaller than people easily disproves that notion. Another common misconception about dinosaurs is that they dragged their tails along the ground behind them, as lizards do. Paleontologists have shown that in reality most dinosaurs carried their tails well off and almost parallel to the ground.

Still another persistent misunderstanding is that most of the creatures that lived in the so-called age of dinosaurs, including monstrous beasts that flew and swam, were dinosaurs. The truth, however, is that *dinosaur* is a very specialized term describing a specific kind of upright-walking land creature. None of the flying reptiles of that prehistoric age were dinosaurs. Similarly, with the exception of *Spinosaurus*, which sometimes hunted in shallow coastal waters, none of the marine reptiles of that long-ago era were dinosaurs.

Nevertheless, when listing the deadliest predators of that age, it is hard to resist including the biggest carnivorous hunter of all times, even if technically it was not a dinosaur. The frightening beast in question is often called Predator X. That was the informal name that experts gave it when they first found its remains in 2006 and still lacked enough information to give it a technical classification and scientific name. In the summer of that year, Norwegian paleontologists unearthed the bones on Svalbard, a Norwegian island group located about 800 miles (1,300 km) from the North Pole. At first, they knew little more than that the creature had roamed the seas about 150 million years ago.

The Seas' Top Predator

Eventually, however, it became clear that Predator X was a kind of plesiosaur, a name that means "ribbon reptile." The plesiosaurs were meat-eating monsters of the deep that ranged in length from as few as 10 feet (3 m) to as many as 60 feet (18 m). Most had serpent-like necks making up half or more of their total length, as well as long tails. Using their tiny, sharp teeth, these marine hunters lived on diets of fish, turtles, and various marine reptiles and amphibians.

Predator X did not have a long neck, however, because it belonged to a small but important group of plesiosaurs having short necks and very large heads. These were the pliosaurs, a Latin name meaning "more lizards." Because Norwegian researchers Bjorn and May-Liss Funke initially found Predator X's remains, scientists assigned it the official name *Pliosaurus funkei* in their honor.

Whatever one chooses to call this remarkable beast, in the Late Jurassic and Early Cretaceous periods it appears to have been the apex predator of the planet's seas. Because most of what is known about it comes

A pliosaur, one of a group of
meat-eating marine monsters
to which Predator X belongs,
attacks a long-necked plesiosaur.
Predator X was likely a top sea
predator thanks to its large teeth
and jaws, its keen sense of smell,
and its immense speed.

from just two partial skeletons, it remains a bit unclear exactly how large it could grow. Estimates range from 40 feet (12 m) to 50 feet (15 m), of which an amazingly large proportion was its head and jaws. Its jaws may have been 8 feet (2.4 m) long, and some scientists speculate that its bite was up to four times more powerful than that of a *T. rex*. "They were the top predators of the sea," University of Alaska Museum scholar Patrick Druckenmiller says of Predator X. He adds that it "had teeth that would have made a *T. rex* whimper."[21]

Hunting Advantages

That Predator X possessed huge jaws filled with large teeth was undoubtedly a major factor in its success as a hunter. Yet there were several other factors that ensured its hunting prowess, of which one was its speed. Scientists estimate that in spite of its great bulk—comparable to some modern whales—the creature was streamlined and agile and could swim up to 16 feet (5 m) per second. Few, if any, other marine animals of that era could outswim it.

Another hunting advantage Predator X enjoyed was a phenomenally good sense of smell. Examinations of the creature's skull show that it was equipped with special internal nostrils that connected with the back of its mouth. When water ahead of the animal streamed back through its mouth, some of the liquid entered those highly sensitive nostrils. There thousands of delicate cells detected any scents of potential prey that might be floating in the nearby water.

Still another factor that made *Pliosaurus funkei* a formidable hunter was its attack strategy, which was at least

- **Scientific name:** *Pliosaurus funkei*
- **Scientific suborder:** Pliosauroidea
- **Scientific family:** Pliosaurid
- **Range:** Worldwide
- **Habitat:** Shallow seas along coastal shelves
- **Average size:** 40 to 50 feet (12 to 15 m) long
- **Diet:** Fish and other marine creatures
- **Life span:** Unknown
- **Key features:** Big flippers for swimming, huge jaws filled with sharp teeth
- **Deadly because:** Fast and strong, with a powerful, crushing bite

sometimes based on stealth tactics. Paleontologists know this thanks to some revealing evidence uncovered in 1981 in Queensland, Australia. It consists of the bones of an *Eromangasaurus*, a genus of long-necked plesiosaur. The skull is badly crushed and partially separated from the body. "When the fossil was examined," Cavan Scott writes, "the cause of death became clear. The *Eromangasaur* seems to have been killed after suffering a devastating bite from a large pliosaur, a bite that severed the head from the rest of its body."[22]

At the time, it was not possible to determine which species of pliosaur had killed the long-necked swimmer. But after the discovery of Predator X almost three decades later, it became clear that a member of its species had been the culprit. Moreover, the experts who studied the damage on the skull were able to determine the angle at which the attacker's jaws clamped down on the victim. In turn, this showed the direction from which the pliosaur approached its prey—from below.

Being a strong, agile swimmer helped Predator X's prowess as a hunter. Pictured are fossil bones from the rear flipper of a pliosaur, the group to which Predator X belongs.

SURVIVORS OF THE GREAT EXTINCTION?

Paleontologists believe that all large animals that existed in the world in Late Cretaceous times died in the massive extinction caused by the K-T event. As near as they can tell, no members of the pliosaur species often called Predator X survived and carried on their line. But a few researchers point to the possibility that a handful of large plesiosaurs might have escaped the catastrophe. If so, they would have needed to be living in a very deep mountain lake or other highly protected geographic location when the disaster struck. This speculation underlies the theory that the so-called Loch Ness monster might be part of a small colony of surviving plesiosaurs that were fairly close relatives of Predator X. Loch Ness is an extremely deep lake in north-central Scotland. Although over the past few centuries hundreds of people swore they saw a large animal swimming there, most scientists argue that evidence for the creature's existence is thin at best. However, in 2003 a tourist found an old bone in the loch, and Scottish scientist Lyall Anderson confirmed that it belonged to a plesiosaur. The unanswered question remains whether that beast dwelled in Loch Ness before or after the great extinction.

It is not surprising, some scientists say, that Predator X employed this devious tactic to ambush its prey. They point out that when possible, great white sharks also assault their victims from below. One possible reason for this is that great whites occupy a similar position in today's food chain to that of Predator X in the Late Jurassic and Early Cretaceous food chain. That position can be described as a very large marine predator equipped with a huge jaw, many sharp teeth, and a crushing, lethal bite.

Seeking Refuge from Predator X

The fact that Predator X routinely attacked large swimming reptiles, including its long-necked plesiosaur cousins, shows that it was the leading predator of the seas in its day. That means that no aquatic creature was safe from its deadly jaws. Besides large and small reptiles, its diet must have also consisted of fish of all sizes, large sea turtles, early crocodiles, and the early versions of today's giant squid.

Considering that members of the savage Predator X species patrolled the seas, paleontologists have addressed the issue of why it did not quickly eliminate long-necked plesiosaurs and other large marine animals. Why, for instance, did Predator X not eat all these competing species' young, causing their kind to go extinct? The conclusion experts have reached is that *Pliosaurus funkei*'s major prey survived by seeking refuge in places that it could not go.

Indeed, although Predator X's enormous bulk, including its massive head and jaws, worked to its advantage in deep waters, its monstrous size worked against it in the shallow waters along the coasts. In coastal lagoons only a few feet deep, its underside would have nearly dragged along the bottom. Put simply, therefore, it could not swim, maneuver well, and hunt in such shallow waters. As a result, smaller aquatic creatures frequented these waters to have and raise their young in relative safety.

A number of scientific discoveries made in the past two or three decades have confirmed the reality of this scenario. Most revealing of all was an expedition to the remote Antarctic island of Vega in 2005. There a team of Argentine and American paleontologists uncovered the bones of many young long-necked plesiosaurs in layers of earth that had been part of coastal shallows in Early Cretaceous times. Also found there were full and partial skeletons of juveniles from numerous other marine species that Predator X preyed on. As one researcher surmises, "This lagoon was a nursery, a protected area where plesiosaurs came to give birth to their babies. It seems reasonable to assume that the young remained in

As with other pliosaurs, Predator X had a massive head and jaws. Pictured is a fossilized pliosaur jaw, the largest such sample ever found. The skull of this ferocious predator measures 7.8 feet (2.4 m) in length.

the safety of the shallows until they grew large enough to face the perils of the open sea."[23]

The Irresistible Urge to Eat

Exactly how long Predator X and other large pliosaurs terrorized the seas remains unknown. What is more certain is that they could not have survived the great mass extinction that occurred 65 million years ago. Dubbed the "K-T event" by scientists, it wiped out not only the land-based dinosaurs (excluding the early ancestors of birds), but also all the large flying and swimming reptiles. The latter included both the long-necked plesiosaurs like *Eromangasaurus* and the short-necked ones like Predator X.

The K-T event was a humungous catastrophe caused by the impact of an asteroid or comet that struck the seabed just off the coast of what is now Mexico's Yucatán Peninsula. Equivalent to more than 1 billion atomic bombs exploding at once, the blast caused massive airborne shock waves and tsunamis and set every forest on Earth ablaze. Even worse, so much dirt and dust was thrown into the atmosphere that sunlight was blocked long enough to kill most vegetation that had survived the fires. This in turn caused most of the planet's food chain to collapse, and all creatures weighing more than 53 pounds (24 kg) went extinct.

The biggest, deadliest beasts of the age of the dinosaurs were gone. Yet soon the survivors of the upheaval began evolving in new directions. Many new lethal hunters would emerge over time, among them poisonous snakes, scorpions, lions, polar bears, and great white sharks. The stark truth is that all creatures in all ages are driven by the irresistible urge to eat. So deadly predators and their prey will always exist because nature demands it.

Source Notes

Chapter 1: Tyrannosaurus Rex

1. Cavan Scott, *Planet Dinosaur: The Next Generation of Killer Giants.* Buffalo, NY: Firefly, 2012, p. 90.
2. David A. Thomas and James O. Farlow, "Tracking a Dinosaur Attack," in *The Scientific American Book of Dinosaurs*, ed. Gregory S. Paul. New York: St. Martin's, 2000, p. 244.
3. Mason Inman, "*T. Rex* Plodded like an Elephant, Nerve Study Says," *National Geographic*, June 30, 2010. http://news.nationalgeographic.com.
4. Mark Strauss, "*Tyrannosaurus Rex:* Armed and Dangerous," *Smithsonian*, October 8, 2008. www.smithsonianmag.com.

Chapter 2: Carcharodontosaurus

5. Scott, *Planet Dinosaur*, p. 63.
6. Scott, *Planet Dinosaur*, p. 63.

Chapter 3: Spinosaurus

7. Quoted in Rebecca Morelle, "*Spinosaurus* Fossil: Giant 'Swimming Dinosaur' Unearthed," BBC, September 11, 2014. www.bbc.com.
8. Quoted in Morelle, "Spinosaurus Fossil."
9. Scott, *Planet Dinosaur*, p. 77.
10. Ellie Zolfagharifard, "Terrifying 'Swimming Dinosaur' Unearthed: Fossils of 97-Million-Year-Old *Spinosaurus* Reveal Giant Predator Ate Sharks Whole," *Daily Mail Online*, September 11, 2014. www.dailymail.co.uk.

11. Quoted in Claire G. Jones, "Scientists Report First Semiaquatic Dinosaur, *Spinosaurus*," *National Geographic*, September 11, 2014. http://press.national geographic.com.

Chapter 4: Troodon

12. Scott, *Planet Dinosaur*, p. 117.
13. Alan D. Gishlick, "Predatory Behavior in Maniraptoran Theropods," in *Paleobiology II*, ed. Derek Briggs and Peter K. Crowther. New York: Wiley, 2008, p. 414.
14. Gishlick, "Predatory Behavior in Maniraptoran Theropods," pp. 414–15.
15. AreXenosDinos?, "*Troodon* vs. Velociraptor," Dinosaur Home, 2015. www.dinosaurhome.com.

Chapter 5: Sinornithosaurus

16. Fran Dorey, "Dinosaurs on the Attack," Australian Museum, 2016. http://australianmuseum.net.au.
17. Quoted in Henry Fountain, "Add Venom to Arsenal of Dinosaurs on the Hunt," *New York Times*, December 29, 2009. www.nytimes.com.
18. DinoFights, "*Sinornithosaurus* vs *Buitreraptor*," Scified, May 22, 2013. www.scified.com.
19. DinoFights, "*Sinornithosaurus* vs *Buitreraptor*."
20. Quoted in CBC News, "Predatory Dinosaur Fed on Smaller Versions of Itself," August 31, 2012. www.cbc.ca.

Chapter 6: Predator X

21. Quoted in Tia Ghose, "Ancient 'Predator X' Sea Monster Gets Official Name," LiveScience, October 17, 2012. www.livescience.com.
22. Scott, *Planet Dinosaur*, p. 139.
23. Scott, *Planet Dinosaur*, p. 138.

apex: The top of something; often used to describe the largest and/or most successful creature that lived in a certain place or time.

biped: A creature that walks on two legs, like a human. Thus, *bipedal* means walking on two legs.

carnivorous: Feeding on meat.

encephalization quotient: Also called EQ, a formula used to compare the brain size of one animal to that of another animal.

extinct: No longer in existence.

geologic time: A term often used to denote the long ages of Earth's history, which have been revealed in various rock layers by geologists.

herbivorous: Feeding on plants.

K-T event: Short for Cretaceous-Tertiary event, the awful catastrophe that ended the Cretaceous period and began the Tertiary period 65 million years ago. It consisted of the collision of a comet or asteroid with Earth. (Scientists use a *K* instead of a *C* for *Cretaceous* because the original name for that period was the German term *Kreide.*)

marine: Dwelling in water.

paleontologists: Scientists who dig up and study ancient life forms.

predator: An animal that hunts and eats another.

prehistoric: Before writing; the term is often used to describe the world and the creatures in it long before humans came on the scene.

theropod: A carnivorous dinosaur that walked on two legs and had small forelimbs, large jaws, and many sharp teeth.

For Further Research

Books

Juan C. Alanso and Gregory S. Paul, *Ancient Earth Journal: The Early Cretaceous.* Minneapolis, MN: Foster, 2015.

Editors of DK Publishing, *Dinosaur!* New York: Dorling Kindersley and Smithsonian, 2014.

Editors of DK Publishing, *Dinosaurs: A Visual Encyclopedia.* New York: Dorling Kindersley, 2011.

Paul Harrison, *Deadly Predators, the Most Dangerous That Ever Lived.* London: Arcturus, 2012.

Paul Harrison, *Terrifying T-Rex and Other Mighty Meat Eaters!* London: Arcturus, 2012.

Hugo Nakikov, *Spinosaurus.* North Hobart, Australia: Severed, 2015.

Gregory S. Paul, *The Princeton Field Guide to Dinosaurs.* Princeton, NJ: Princeton University Press, 2010.

Cavan Scott, *Planet Dinosaur: The Next Generation of Killer Giants.* Buffalo, NY: Firefly, 2012.

Brian Switek and Julius Csotonyi, *Prehistoric Predators.* New York: Applesauce, 2015.

C.J. Waller, *Predator X.* North Hobart, Australia: Severed, 2014.

Internet Sources

Biz Carson, "New Giant Dinosaur Was the Apex Predator Before *T-Rex*," *Wired*, November 22, 2013. www.wired.com/2013/11/new-dinosaur-siats.

Prehistoric Wildlife, "Top Ten Predatory Dinosaurs." www.prehistoric-wildlife.com/top-tens/top-ten-predatory-dinosaurs.html.

Reuters, "'Chicken from Hell' Found Who Lived Alongside *T-Rex*," *Haaretz* (Tel Aviv, Israel), March 20, 2014. www.haaretz.com/israel-news/science/1.580901.

Ruth Schuster and Will Dunham, "Dinosaur Bigger than *T-Rex* Found—and It Hunted in Water," *Haaretz* (Tel Aviv, Israel), September 14, 2014. www.haaretz.com/israel-news/science/1.615662.

Bob Strauss, "The Ten Deadliest Dinosaurs," About.com, 2016. http://dinosaurs.about.com/od/dinosaurbasics/ss/The-10-Deadliest-Dinosaurs.htm.

Websites

BBC, Nature: Dinosaurs (www.bbc.co.uk/nature/14343366). The prestigious British Broadcasting Corporation produced this fulsome site about dinosaurs, which features sections on dinosaurs becoming birds, how dinosaurs hunted, what they ate, how they are named, the cause of their extinction, and which ones were the deadliest.

Dinosauria (www.ucmp.berkeley.edu/diapsids/dinosaur.html). Maintained by the California Museum of Paleontology and containing numerous fact-filled pages, this is one of the better sources of information about dinosaurs on the Internet.

Enchanted Learning: Zoom Dinosaurs (www.enchant edlearning.com/subjects/dinosaurs/). Geared toward younger readers this site contains numerous pages filled with useful information, including a list of dinosaurs, discussions of dinosaur behavior, and introductions to leading paleontologists.

Index

Note: Boldface page numbers indicate illustrations.

Picture Credits

Cover: Shutterstock.com/Bob Orsillo

6: Depositphotos

9: Depositphotos

13: Side profile of a tyrannosaurus rex in the forest (photo)/ De Agostini Picture Library/Bridgeman Images

16: © Corbis

19: Associated Press

23: Shutterstock.com/Ryan M. Bolton

26: Carcharodontosaurus guards its kill against deltadromeus (colour litho), Hallett, Mark (20th Century)/ National Geographic Creative/Bridgeman Images

31: © Bao Dandan/Xinhua Press/Corbis

32: Depositphotos

35: © Kay Nietfeld/dpa/Corbis

39: Troodon (colour litho)/Natural History Museum, London, UK/Bridgeman Images

41: Laurie O'Keefe/Science Photo Library

45: Illustration of Troodon catching young dinosaurs from nest (photo)/De Agostini Picture Library/Bridgeman Images

48: Sinornithosaurus/Natural History Museum, London, UK/ Bridgeman Images

52: Laurie O'Keefe/Science Photo Library

55: David Burnham/Newscom

59: © National Geographic Creative/Corbis

62: Natural History Museum, London/Science Photo Library

65: Associated Press

Historian and award-winning writer Don Nardo has published more than four hundred books for teens and children, along with a number of volumes for college and general adult readers. He specializes in the Greeks, Romans, Egyptians, and other ancient peoples; and some of his books delve back even further, into the prehistoric world of the dinosaurs and other extinct beasts. Nardo, who also composes and arranges orchestral music, lives with his wife, Christine, in Massachusetts.